AR PTS: 1.0

Nature's Fury

WILDFIRES

John Hamilton

ABDO
& Daughters

VISIT US AT

WWW.ABDOPUB.COM

Published by ABDO Publishing Company, 4940 Viking Drive, Suite 622, Edina, Minnesota 55435.
Copyright ©2006 by Abdo Consulting Group, Inc. International copyrights reserved in all countries.
No part of this book may be reproduced in any form without written permission from the publisher.
ABDO & Daughters™ is a trademark and logo of ABDO Publishing Company.

Printed in the United States.

Editor: Paul Joseph

Graphic Design: John Hamilton

Cover Design: Neil Klinepier

Cover Photo: Corbis

Interior Photos and Illustrations:

 Corbis, p. 1, 3, 4, 5, 6, 7, 8-9, 10-11, 12, 13, 14, 15, 16, 17, 18, 26, 27, 28, 29, 32
 Hinckley Fire Museum, p. 21, 22, 23, 24, 25

Library of Congress Cataloging-in-Publication Data

Hamilton, John, 1959–
    Wildfires / John Hamilton.
        p. cm. — (Nature's fury)
        Includes index.
    ISBN 1-59679-330-9
    1. Wildfires—Juvenile literature. I. Title.

    SD421.23.H36 2006
    363.37'9—dc22
                                                    2005040422

CONTENTS

A firefighter rests after battling a blaze in California's Yosemite National Park in 1995.

WILDFIRE!

IT CAN BEGIN WITH THE LITTLEST THING: A GLOWING EMBER from a campfire floating in the wind, a cigarette tossed carelessly out a car window, even a stray spark born by a train's metal wheel striking a track. But from this tiny beginning springs one of nature's most fearsome forces: wildfire!

With the right conditions, small flames can grow into fiery monsters that consume everything in their path. Forests and grasslands become powder kegs that burst into flames, destroying millions of acres of land, burning houses and businesses, and snatching away the lives of unfortunate victims.

Each year in the United States, appoximately 100,000 wildfires burn about 5 million acres (2 million hectares) of land. Although lightning starts many fires, four out of five are caused by human activity. Usually carelessness is the cause, but sometimes people set fires on purpose, a serious crime called arson.

A house burns near San Diego, CA, in October, 2003.

Despite the danger and destruction, naturalists today know that fire is a very important part of the ecosystem. It clears out dense underbrush and helps many kinds of trees and animals to thrive. But as people's homes and businesses spread out from the cities into the nation's woodlands, fire is becoming a more common threat.

Wildfires can send sheets of flame over the countryside at a frightening rate of speed, giving people little time to react. Each year more and more people, if they're lucky enough to survive, find their hopes and dreams replaced with smoldering ruins.

Firefighters watch a fire burn out of control at Simi Valley, CA, during southern California's record-setting fire season of 2003.

THE SCIENCE OF WILDFIRES

WILDFIRES ARE OFTEN CALLED WILDLAND FIRES BY THE PEOPLE who study them. Wildland fires include forest fires, brush fires, and scrub fires—any wilderness area outside of a city or suburb. The U.S. government's Federal Emergency Management Agency (FEMA) classifies wildland fires into three types.

Surface fires are the most common. Open flames burn material on the floor of a forest. If a surface fire moves slowly, it can kill or damage trees. *Ground fires* are often started by lightning. They burn on or just below the forest floor, feeding on dead vegetation that has built up over the years. *Crown fires* burn on the tops, or canopy, of forests. When the wind is blowing, crown fires can jump along from treetop to treetop.

Fire marches up a ridge near Carlsbad, CA, in 1996.

Wildfires strike in many parts of the world, especially where climates allow the growth of trees and grasses, but where dry periods are common. During the hot days of summer fallen branches, leaves, and other vegetation dry out and become flammable. The grasslands and scrublands of Australia, the United States, and Canada are especially at risk for wildfires. In Australia, wildfires are called *bushfires*.

A pine tree is engulfed in flames by a fast-moving brush fire.

Every material, whether it's a twig, a piece of paper, or a tree trunk, has a *flashpoint*. This is the temperature at which the material will burst into flames. The flashpoint of wood is 572 degrees Fahrenheit (300 C). When wood is heated to this temperature, it begins to release hydrocarbon gas, which then mixes with the oxygen in the air. This volatile mixture then combusts and creates fire.

Heat, oxygen, and fuel are the three critical parts needed to keep a wildfire alive. These three parts are called the *fire triangle*. Fuel feeds the flames, air supplies the oxygen, and a source of heat brings the fuel up to its flashpoint. When faced with an out-of-control wildfire, firefighters keep in mind the fire triangle. If just one of the three critical elements is suppressed, a fire can be stopped dead in its tracks.

On the other hand, one of the three elements might get stronger. For example, if winds suddenly increase and supply the fire with a richer source of oxygen, then a small fire can easily turn into a raging inferno.

Wildfires burn a forest near Glenwood Springs, CO, in June, 2002.

A bushfire consumes dry grasses in Kakadu National Park, Australia.

Once a fire begins, there are three things that will help it spread: *weather*, *fuel*, and *topography*. Weather is extremely important. Unfortunately, it is something nobody can control. Many wildfires continue to burn until late autumn or even until winter weather sets in. Cold air makes it harder for fuels to reach their flashpoint.

Rain is another important weather factor that helps firefighters. Rain covers the surface of the fuel (trees, brush, leaves, etc.), temporarily cutting it off from the surrounding air and its oxygen supply. Also, moisture soaks into the fuel supply. Water inside a plant or piece of wood absorbs a lot of heat as it evaporates. This is why a wet piece of wood takes longer to catch fire. It must dry out first before it can be heated to its flashpoint.

Wildfires are much more common during drought years, when vegetation has very little moisture inside. Even

water in the air can affect a wildfire. When there is high humidity, water vapor in the air absorbs heat, suppressing fire. But when humidity is low, wildfires are more likely to start.

As we have seen, weather affects the flammability of a fire's fuel supply. But what exactly is fuel? Fuel is basically anything that will burn and feed the flames. In wildland fires, this is most often underbrush, grasses, and trees. The amount of this kind of material that is available to burn is called a fire's *fuel load*. The bigger the fuel load, the more intense a wildfire may grow. Areas with sparse grasses or vegetation have light fuel loads. These fires often burn slowly, with low intensity. Forests with large amounts of underbrush, such as dried twigs and leaves on the forest floor, have very heavy fuel loads. These fires can burn very quickly and intensely, spreading rapidly by heating up the areas around them. And the drier the fuel, the

A firefighter watches helplessly as an out-of-control wildfire races up a hillside.

faster the fire spreads, making it very difficult for firefighters to contain.

Some kinds of materials are called *flashy fuels*. These include such things as pine needles, twigs, and dried grasses and leaves. Flashy fuels go up in flames very quickly. A flashy fuel is something that doesn't have much weight compared to its surface area. This is why it's easy to start a sheet of paper on fire with a single match, but it takes much longer to set a wood log ablaze. Woodlands with a lot of flashy fuels on the forest floor can be very susceptible to wildfires. Sometimes even the summer heat from the sun can start a fire by igniting flashy fuel, especially if it's dried out from a drought.

A fire tornado rises from a wildfire in southern California.

Topography, or the shape of the land, is the third element that determines how a fire spreads. Firefighters have their biggest challenge in mountainous areas. Fires travel uphill very quickly. Heat from fires at the bottom of a mountain dries out areas higher up the slope, and then preheats the fuel to make it burst into flames very quickly. Steeper slopes usually mean faster-spreading fires. Many firefighters have been killed because they were unable to outrun wildfires racing up mountainsides.

Wildfires, even those not on mountains, can spread at frightening speeds. With the right wind conditions, some fires can spread up to 40 miles (64 km) in a single day, devouring up to 1,000 acres (405 hectares) of wildland each hour. Tremendous heat and clouds of hot embers push ahead of the main wall of flame, leapfrogging over man-made firebreaks and natural barriers such as rivers.

Extreme fires behave in bizarre, unpredictable ways, sometimes even creating their own weather. Large, intense fires burn so much fuel that they suck in air from surrounding areas. These heavy winds fuel the flames and can create firestorms and firewhirls, tornados of fire that can hurl flaming debris great distances.

FIGHTING FIRES

FOR MANY YEARS, THE POLICY OF THE UNITED STATES WAS TO fight and extinguish every wildfire. But many forests need fire to stay healthy. The cones of jack pine trees release seeds only when exposed to intense heat. Fire also clears out deadwood and other material, giving plants and trees room to grow. This helps animals to thrive as well. And forests that have been exposed to fire are more resistant to drought and insect invasions.

Over the years, the policy of stopping all fires led to a buildup of dead material on many forest floors. This led to more intense and damaging fires than would have happened naturally. Since the 1960's, the U.S. Forest Service has let many fires burn themselves out, recognizing that fire is a natural part of the ecosystem. Fires caused by lightning that start in remote areas are usually allowed to burn. The Forest Service even sets some fires deliberately under carefully controlled conditions. These are called *prescribed fires*. By getting rid of excessive dead material on the forest floor, the Forest Service hopes to avoid larger, more destructive fires in the future.

Sometimes prescribed fires can go terribly wrong. Shifting weather conditions make fires behave unpredictably. In the summer

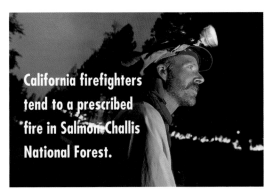

California firefighters tend to a prescribed fire in Salmon-Challis National Forest.

A firefighter manages
a bushfire in Australia.

A smokejumper parachutes into a remote wilderness area.

of 2000, a prescribed fire in New Mexico went out of control, eventually burning more than 45,000 acres (18,200 hectares) of wilderness. The fire threatened to destroy the U.S. nuclear weapons facility at Los Alamos, New Mexico, before it finally subsided.

To fight wildfires that rage out of control and threaten lives and property, the Forest Service uses 20-person teams called *hotshots*. These are highly trained firefighters who build *firebreaks* to keep flames from spreading. Using specially designed axes, shovels, and chainsaws, hotshot crews clear lines of deadwood and other possible fuel ahead of a line of fire. Once the fire reaches the firebreak, it has no fuel left and burns itself out. In addition to creating firebreaks, firefighters also use water and fire retardants to cool down hot spots. Hotshots also cause *backfires* ahead of the main fire. Backfires are small

controlled burns that eliminate much of the potential fuel ahead of the main line of fire. Firefighters use drip torches to start backfires.

Sometimes it is very difficult to send fire crews into remote areas. Smokejumpers are specially trained firefighters who parachute out of airplanes. They are sent into remote wilderness areas to suppress smaller fires before they can grow into large wildland fires. It is a very dangerous job. There are only a few hundred smokejumpers in the United States.

In addition to using fire crews on the ground, the Forest Service uses airpower to fight fires. Helicopters use large buckets to drop hundreds of gallons of water on fires. Helicopters are also very useful in transporting fire crews and their equipment.

The biggest weapon in the Forest Service's arsenal is a fleet of air tankers that can drop thousands of gallons of water or retardant directly onto wildfires. Fire retardant is a pink-colored liquid that contains phosphate fertilizer. (It is colored pink to give the pilot a clear idea of where it lands.) Fire retardant, if dropped on target, can greatly help cool and slow down wildfires.

An air tanker drops a load of colored fire retardant.

THE GREAT PESHTIGO FIRE

MOST PEOPLE KNOW ABOUT THE CHICAGO, ILLINOIS, FIRE OF 1871, which may have been started when a cow kicked over a lantern on the night of October 8. But few people know about another fire that began that same day.

The Chicago fire got most of the newspaper coverage, but the Great Peshtigo Fire of 1871 was the deadliest wildfire in U.S. history. Approximately 1,500 people died, and over 1.5 million acres (607,029 hectares) were burned.

Peshtigo, Wisconsin, was a wood-manufacturing center in 1871, just north of Green Bay. That summer was especially dry. On the night of October 8, hot winds caused many smaller fires to combine into one gigantic forest fire. Many people were caught unprepared. Thick smoke made it hard to see even a few feet ahead. The tremendous heat caused treetops to ignite. Firewhirls, small tornados of flame, shot hot cinders and debris far ahead of the main blaze. One eyewitness wrote, "Great volumes of fire would rise up, fifty feet from the top of the trees, leap over thirty acres of clearing and, in an instant, flame up in the forests beyond."

The fire produced its own convection currents as it consumed oxygen and fuel, creating hurricane-force winds. Buildings and people literally burst into flames. Others died of asphyxiation, or were boiled alive in shallow marshes or wells. Those who survived fled the worst of the fire and spent the night in deep rivers or ponds.

Many communities in the Green Bay area were damaged. The city of Peshtigo was completely burned to the ground. More than 800 people died in Peshtigo alone—more than half the town's population.

An illustration showing people escaping the firestorm of the Peshtigo blaze of 1871.

THE HINCKLEY FIRE OF 1894

THE SUMMER OF 1894 WAS ONE OF THE DRIEST ON RECORD IN the upper Midwest. In small logging towns across northern Minnesota, people sweltered in the sun as they went about their business. New settlements across the northern plains demanded white pine, which made logging the king of the Minnesota's economy.

In those days, logging practices were wasteful. Lumber mills only wanted the trunks of trees. The tops and branches were left on the ground. This waste material was called slash. It became very dry and could catch fire easily, even from the spark of a train's metal wheels. Small brush fires were common. Smoke often filled the air.

On September 1, 1894, several slash fires combined and began rampaging across the state. The fire raced faster than a galloping horse, scorching about 256,000 acres (103,600 hectares) in four hours. The logging town of Hinckley, Minnesota, was hardest hit. The fire also burned the towns of Sandstone, Mission Creek, Pokegama, Miller, and Askov. The fire was so huge that witnesses as far south as Iowa reported seeing the inferno's glow. By the end of the day, the fire had killed 413 people.

When the town of Hinckley was engulfed by the firestorm, many fled in terror. Those who stayed behind were burned alive. North of the town were small swamps, where some people sought refuge from the flames. One survivor wrote, "As we got in the water a bunch of confused deer raced past us right into the blast that roared over us in seconds. One man was in the middle

The smoking ruins of Hinckley, Minnesota, after the fire of 1894. This view shows all that is left of the town's train station.

A flooded gravel pit where some of the survivors found shelter from the flames.

with a wet, course wool sock held over his mouth with his left hand. With his right he splashed water over us and the creek bank. I went under as the water sizzled with the rain of firebrands. That warmed the water and killed the fish in seconds. I breathed through my wet shirt when I came up for air."

Other people weren't so lucky. In one shallow swamp 127 people were killed when a firewhirl swept over the area, asphyxiating them or boiling them alive.

One mile north of Hinckley, a group of 150 people, many of them women and children, were stumbling along a train track, desperately trying to stay ahead of the flames. Suddenly, a train appeared out of the smoky darkness. It was the southbound No. 4 out of Duluth, Minnesota. The engineer was James Root, who stopped the train as soon as he saw the horrific scene ahead of him. The people from Hinckley quickly boarded the train.

Root waited as long as he could for stragglers to catch the train, but soon the firestorm was almost upon them. When the railroad ties under the train caught fire, Root knew it was time to go. He could no longer go toward the doomed

Engineer James Root's locomotive.

James Root

town of Hinckley, so Root threw the train in reverse. They would have to go back through the fiery woods to reach safety.

Root knew there was a lake about five miles (8 km) to their north, but he didn't know if they could make it in time. Firewhirls shot flaming debris on both sides of the train. Engineer Root kept his hands gripped on the metal throttle lever, his hands blistering in the heat. When Root's clothes caught fire, one of his assistants threw buckets of water on Root and his crew to help

cool them down. Glass on a cab window burst in the heat. A shard lodged in Root's neck, close to the jugular vein. Weak from loss of blood and the tremendous heat, Root somehow managed to keep the train running.

Finally they arrived at the shores of Skunk Lake. Engineer Root stopped the train and the panicked passengers leapt off, stumbling through the ash and blinding smoke toward the murky waters of the lake. John Blair, a porter on the train, heroically helped many passengers reach safety.

Engineer Root was too weak to go by himself. His crew pried his hands from the lever, shocked to see that most of his skin was stuck to the hot iron. Root's eyebrows and most of his hair were burned off, and his face was full of heat blisters. They dragged him to the lake as fire swirled all around them.

Waves of fire blasted over the people in the lake. The oven-like air was choked with smoke and searing embers. Fire tornadoes roared overhead, causing the tops of trees to explode like fiery grenades. If the train passengers hadn't found shelter in the cool deep waters of Skunk Lake they surely would have burned to death. After many terrifying minutes, the fire began to subside. The Great Hinckley Fire of 1894 was finally burning itself out.

Hinckley's school was the only building in town left partially standing after the fire.

A search party looks for bodies in the ruins of a burned cabin.

Engineer James Root's actions that day saved more than 300 people. Miraculously, he made a full recovery. He eventually returned to his old railroad job.

Despite this and other stories of heroism, more than 400 people lost their lives in the inferno. Hinckley and other small towns were completely burned to the ground. It would take many years for them to rebuild. A monument stands today in Hinckley, dedicated to "The Pioneers of Civilization in the Forests of Minnesota."

Steps were taken in the logging industry to reduce the amount of slash and waste products that fed the fire, so that another tragedy like the one that struck Hinckley would never happen again.

THE YELLOWSTONE FIRES OF 1988

FIRES ARE A NATURAL PART OF FOREST AND GRASSLAND ecosystems. By fighting every fire that it could in the first part of the 20th century, the U.S. Forest Service created a landscape where forests had accumulated layers of deadwood, dried leaves, and pine needles, ready to go up in flames.

The summer of 1988 was hot and dry in the American West. In August, 13 major fires, most of them started by lightning but some by careless humans, converged and swept through large parts of Yellowstone National Park in Wyoming. Fanned by high winds, sheets of flames reached hundreds of feet high, leapfrogging over firebreaks and raging out of control. The fires burned an estimated 988,925 acres (400,204 hectares) of parkland.

The Forest Service sent thousands of firefighters to combat the blaze. Airplanes dropped more than seven million gallons of retardant, and helicopters dropped 10 million gallons of water, one bucket at a time. Hotshot crews, smokejumpers, and support teams did their best to protect the park's most

Trees go up in flames in Yellowstone.

An air tanker drops a load of fire retardant in an attempt to keep a ridge fire from advancing on a populated area in Yellowstone National Park.

famous landmarks, like Old Faithful Inn. Mostly, however, firefighters were at the mercy of the inferno.

More than 68,000 wildfires scorched the West that summer. The worst of them broke out in Montana. Despite the best efforts of the Forest Service, it was Mother Nature who finally came to the rescue, with late September snowstorms finally extinguishing the wildfires of 1988.

CALIFORNIA 2003

FIFTEEN MAJOR FIRES RAGED OUT OF CONTROL IN LATE OCTOBER 2003, in southern California. The biggest and most destructive of these was the Cedar Fire in central San Diego County. Hot and dry conditions, mixed with stiff Santa Ana winds, created one of the worst natural disasters in the history of California.

For two weeks the southern California blazes brought terror and misery, scorching 721,791 acres (292,098 hectares) of land, killing 24 people, and destroying nearly 4,000 homes. More than 13,000 firefighters were called in to battle the blaze.

Wildfires consume homes in southern California in October, 2003.

The California fires of 2003 were so destructive because of a combination of factors. They all combined to create the perfect conditions for an inferno. Low rainfall and hot weather created drought conditions nearly five years in a row. Grasses and trees were tinder dry. Also, because of fire suppression in times past, there were many years' worth of underbrush built up on the ground. In addition, pine bark beetles had killed millions of trees. The deadwood was dried out and ready to become fuel for wildfires.

Once the fires started, hot, dry winds called Santa Ana's blew in from the desert and fanned the flames. Small fires became raging infernos. After the

Firefighters watch a helicopter make
a water drop over a fire raging in
Simi Valley, California.

Santa Ana's died down, Pacific Ocean winds blew the fires in new directions, spreading them in unpredictable ways.

After two weeks, cooler weather, fog, and drizzle helped firefighters bring the blazes under control. Ash fell like snow for days in some places.

Forestry experts warn that the 2003 wildfires in southern California could easily happen again, given the right conditions. As more and more people build their houses and businesses in fire country, it's only a matter of time before nature's fury will strike again.

GLOSSARY

ARSON

The crime of purposefully setting fire to someone else's land or property. Arsonists also set fire to their own property in order to collect insurance money. Arson is a very serious crime that kills and injures many people, as well as destroys property and public lands.

ECOSYSTEM

A biological community of animals, plants, and bacteria, all of whom live together in the same physical or chemical environment.

FIRE TRIANGLE

The three critical parts needed to create a wildfire. The fire triangle includes fuel to feed the flames, air to supply oxygen, and a heat source to bring the fuel up to its flashpoint. If any of these three elements is taken away, a wildfire can be suppressed.

FLASHPOINT

The temperature at which a material will burst into flames. The flashpoint of wood is 572 degrees Fahrenheit (300 C).

FLASHY FUELS

Material such as pine needles, twigs, and dried grasses, which start on fire very quickly. Flashy fuels don't have much weight compared to their surface area, which allows them to reach their flashpoint much quicker.

Fuel Load

The amount of material, such as underbrush, grasses, and trees, that is available for a fire to consume. Forest fires with a heavy fuel load burn intensely and spread rapidly.

Hotshots

Twenty-person teams of highly trained firefighters that are sent by the United States Forest Service to battle out-of-control wildfires. Hotshot crews are skilled at clearing firebreaks to prevent fires from spreading. They also set controlled backfires ahead of the main fire in order to eliminate potential fuel.

Naturalist

Someone who studies nature by observing animals and plants.

Prescribed Fire

A fire that is set intentionally in order to get rid of excessive dead material on the forest floor. In this way larger, more destructive fires can be prevented. Sometimes prescribed burns can get out of control. The U.S. Forest Service tries to be very careful when setting fires, which can often burn unpredictably. Usually, however, prescribed burns are successfully controlled, and prevent future destruction.

WEB SITES

WWW.ABDOPUB.COM

Would you like to learn more about wildfires? Please visit www.abdopub.com to find up-to-date Web site links about wildfires and other natural disasters. These links are routinely monitored and updated to provide the most current information available.

INDEX

A portrait of California firefighters.